IMAGES
of America

THE
CHARLES
A RIVER TRANSFORMED

IMAGES
of America

THE
CHARLES
A RIVER TRANSFORMED

William P. Marchione, Ph.D.

ARCADIA

First published 1998
Copyright © William P. Marchione, Ph.D., 1998

ISBN 0-7524-0827-5

Published by Arcadia Publishing,
an imprint of the Chalford Publishing Corporation,
One Washington Center, Dover, New Hampshire 03820.
Printed in Great Britain

Library of Congress Cataloging-in-Publication Data applied for

Contents

Acknowledgments

While many books have been written on the history of the Charles River as a whole, none has dealt with the basin exclusively. The present volume is designed to fill that gap.

The Charles: A River Transformed grew out of my work with the Brighton-Allston Historical Society. Some 5 miles of the Charles River wash the northern boundary of Allston-Brighton. The transformation of the Charles from a commercial thoroughfare, lined with factories and lumber wharves, into the area's greatest recreational resource has been a recurrent theme of my lectures, articles, and books on Allston-Brighton history. It was but a short step from a localized perspective to a broader consideration of the basin's history. In recent years, the Brighton-Allston Historical Society has sponsored a number of Charles River Basin cruises, which I have had the privilege of narrating. Many thanks are therefore due the members of that organization for their continuing interest and support of my historical labors.

I wish to acknowledge, in particular, the assistance of my longtime friend Charlie Vasiliades, president of the Brighton-Allston Historical Society, whose contributions to this volume included the loan of historical material, a thorough proofreading of the text, as well as valuable suggestions for improvement.

I would also like to thank the staff of the Watertown Free Public Library for its help in locating a number of the images that appear in this volume.

Thanks is also due Kevin A. McCluskey, Harvard University Director of Community Relations; Brent M. Sverdloff, Reference Archivist of Historical Collections at Harvard's Baker Library; and Harvard University Archivist Harley Holden for their help in locating and obtaining permission to publish the images credited to the Harvard University.

Finally, I would like to thank Jamie Carter of Arcadia Publishing, editor of both of my Arcadia books, for her unfailing courtesy and valuable assistance.

William P. Marchione, Ph.D.
Curator, Brighton-Allston Historical Society

One

Tidal Estuary

Prior to 1908, when the Charles River Improvement Project transformed the character and function of the Charles River Basin, that body of water had an altogether different appearance. In its natural state, the basin was a tidal estuary, an arm of the sea garlanded by hundreds of acres of salt marshes and mudflats which the onrushing and receding tides filled and emptied twice in every 24-hour period. This 9-mile-long tidal estuary extended from the river's mouth at Boston Harbor to a point just above Watertown Square.

In the pre-colonial period, native bands moved into the basin each spring to avail themselves of its fertile soil and abundant fish and game. For thousands of years this bountiful ecosystem sustained and enriched the native culture. Then a devastating plague, brought to the coastal settlements by European trading vessels in the 1616–18 period, decimated the native society, thereby ending the first epoch in the history of the basin.

The earliest authenticated European contacts with the Charles River Basin were those of the French explorer Samuel de Champlain in 1605, and of the English explorer Captain John Smith in 1614. Smith named the river "Massachusetts," after the local native tribe, but Prince Charles of England (later King Charles I) renamed it "The River Charles."

The first European settlers to establish themselves in the area came as part of the great Puritan migration of 1630 that established the Massachusetts Bay Colony. Within a few months of their arrival, these energetic English men and women founded three communities on the shores of the Charles River Basin: Boston, Watertown, and Cambridge.

Boston, which lay on the peninsula that enclosed the basin's southern shore, became the colony's principal trading center. This town's orientation was from the beginning easterly toward the harbor and the sea. Still, the river at its back door served as an important artery of trade linking the goods of the colony's developing interior to Boston's many warehouses and docks.

The economic orientation of Cambridge and Watertown was agricultural rather than commercial. Here lay ample farmland and timber as well as thousands of acres of marsh grasses and pasturage for livestock raising.

Watertown's settlers at first located at Gerry's Landing in present-day Cambridge. Within a few years, however, the settlement's center shifted 4 miles further up river to the site of present-day Watertown Square, where a set of rapids had been harnessed to power a gristmill. Seventeenth-century Watertown also served as the colony's principal gateway to the west, a point of transshipment for those travelling into Massachusetts' developing interior.

Cambridge, the last of the three towns to be founded, was intended as a fortified capital (called at first Newtowne). This plan was shortly abandoned, however, when Governor John Winthrop decided to settle in Boston. The special character of Cambridge derived instead from the establishment there in 1636–38 of Harvard College, the first seat of higher learning in the English colonies.

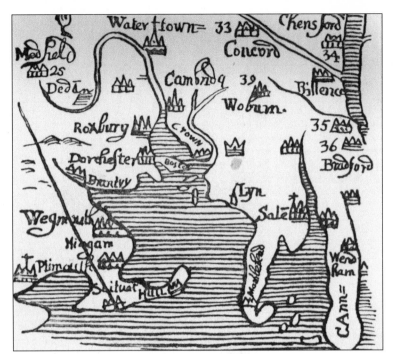

This detail from William Hubbard's 1677 map of New England (the first map printed in the Massachusetts Bay Colony) centers on the Charles River and adjacent towns.

The earliest attempt at settlement on the Charles River Basin occurred in June 1630 when a party (originally from Dorchester, England) under the command of Roger Clap landed on the steep bank behind the present-day Perkins School for the Blind in Watertown. The local natives gave the English a friendly welcome. Since the title to this land was in dispute, however, Governor John Winthrop soon ordered Clap to abandon the location. Moving south of Boston, Clap and his followers founded the Town of Dorchester.

Sir Richard Saltonstall, a principal founder of the Massachusetts Bay Colony and one of only two titled original settlers (the other being Sir Issac Johnson, a founder of Boston), led a group of one hundred Puritan families up the Charles in late July 1630 to Gerry's Landing in present-day Cambridge to found Watertown. Within a year, however, Sir Richard returned to England, where he spent the balance of his life.

Watertown's handsome tercentennial Founder's Monument, erected in 1930, stands on the banks of the Charles River near the intersection of Charles River Road and Riverside Street. It depicts Sir Richard Saltonstall and is decorated with a bas-relief of Clap's earlier landing on the Watertown shore. The Founder's Monument was designed by Henry Hudson Kitson.

This engraving of Copp's Hill in Boston's North End conveys a sense of the rugged character of the landscape in the early years. Copp's Hill and the village of Charlestown on the opposite shore lay at the mouth of the Charles River. The windmill was constructed in 1632, there being no adequate source of waterpower available in Boston. A ferry operating between the foot of Copp's Hill and Winnismet (present-day Chelsea) provided access to the towns north of Boston.

Watertown hired Thomas Mayhew to build a water-powered gristmill east of the rapids at the western end of the tidal basin. A stone wall was built to hold back the flow of water, and an arc-shaped canal was constructed leading to a gate that could be opened or closed to regulate the flow. As the only mill in the general area, the Watertown Grist Mill became a trading focal point and was the chief factor in shifting the center of Watertown. (Courtesy of the Watertown Free Library.)

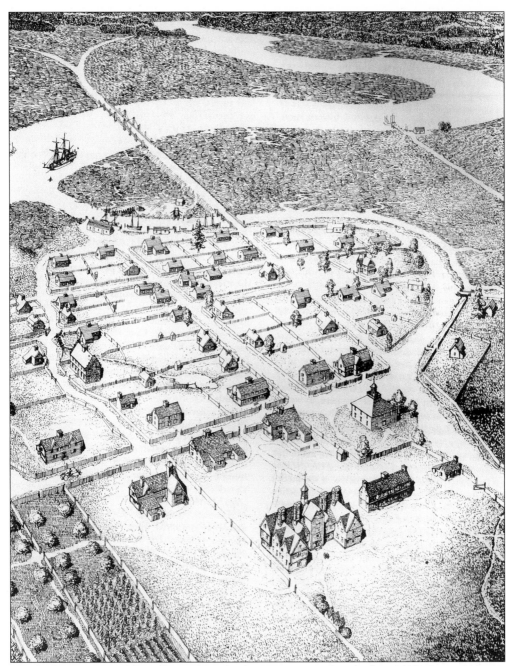

This bird's-eye view of the village of Cambridge as it appeared in the late 1600s shows the great extent of salt marshes that then bordered both sides of the river. The man-made Town Creek, dating from 1632, formed the western boundary of the village. Just west of where it entered the river stood the Great Bridge, constructed in 1662, which connected Cambridge proper to the Roxbury Highway, leading to Boston 8 miles away. Because of the instability of the marshes on the north side of the river, a causeway to dry land was provided. The large building in the foreground is Harvard College, founded in 1636–38. (Courtesy of the Harvard University Archives.)

This 1764 view of the mouth of the Charles River looks north from Beacon Hill in the direction of the North End and Charlestown.

This view of Charlestown looking across the Charles River from Boston's North End comes from a much larger 1770 engraving made by British engineers. The cliff on the right is Copp's Hill. In the distance lies the village of Charlestown.

The British prepared this map of Boston and vicinity in 1775. Notice the absence of bridges on the Charles River east of the so-called Great Bridge at present-day Harvard Square in Cambridge. The topography of the tidal Charles seriously impeded north-south travel. Access to the northern towns by horse or wagon required a journey of some 8 miles to the Great Bridge by way of the Roxbury Neck and the Roxbury Highway through Roxbury, Brookline, and Little Cambridge (present-day Allston-Brighton).

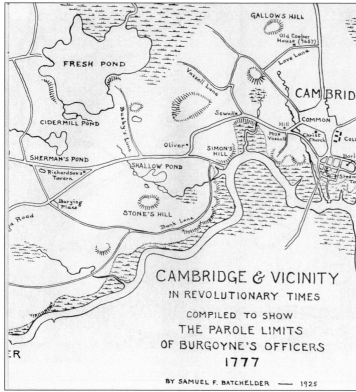

In 1925 Samuel Batchelder drew a map for the Cambridge Historical Society of the Charles River Basin as it appeared in 1777.

13

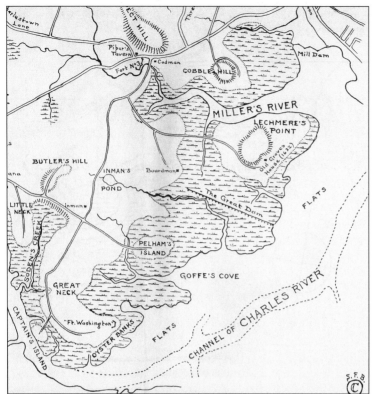

This detail from the Batchelder map shows how extensive the marshes were in the eastern part of the basin. Lechmere Point, in present-day East Cambridge, was a virtual island. Note should also be taken of Fort Washington on the Great Neck in present-day Cambridgeport, one of a number of revolutionary entrenchments built in 1775 during the Siege of Boston.

Here we have a depiction of the most famous incident in the history of the Charles River Basin. Paul Revere arrives on the northern bank of the Charles River in East Cambridge on the night of April 18, 1775, to begin his mythic ride to Lexington to alert the farmers of Middlesex County of the imminent arrival of British troops, the incident that sparks the American Revolution.

During the eleven-month long Siege of Boston (1775–76), a British officer prepared these sketches of the American entrenchments surrounding the town. Both look out over the Charles River Basin from Beacon Hill. Above we have a southwesterly view toward Roxbury and Brookline. Notable details include a British encampment on Boston Common (lower left-hand corner) and the John Hancock Mansion (left center), which stood just west of the present Massachusetts State House. The lower view looks northwesterly toward Cambridge. Details include West Hill (left center), one of the three promontories of Boston's Trimount (now Beacon Hill), and also the ropewalks that then stood on the northern slope of the Trimount.

This engraving, entitled *A View of the Lines Thrown Up on Boston Neck by the Ministerial Army*, was prepared for General Washington during the Siege of Boston. The narrow Roxbury Neck and the western shore of the Boston Peninsula here enclose the Charles River Basin's Back Bay. The original diagram of these entrenchments was prepared by John Trumbull, adjutant of the Connecticut regiment, who later gained fame as the so-called "Painter of the American Revolution."

One of the great battles of the Revolutionary War, the Battle of Bunker Hill, was fought at the mouth of the Charles River on June 17, 1775. At issue was control of the heights north of Boston, within easy cannon range of the British army headquartered there. During the battle, the British artillery atop Copp's Hill in Boston's North End and aboard the warship *Somerset* anchored in the Charles River poured a relentless fire into Charlestown, burning that town to the ground.

This 1791 view of Boston from Breed's Hill in Charlestown includes the Charlestown Bridge (right center), constructed in 1786 at the mouth of the Charles River. Boston was growing rapidly in the late 1780s and early 1790s. Other key details include Boston's crowded North End (left center) and the rapidly developing West End (right), overlooking the tidal basin.

"Elmwood," near Gerry Landing, is one of the great colonial residences of Cambridge. Built in 1769 on the margin of the tidal basin by Loyalist Thomas Oliver, it subsequently served as the residence of Elbridge Gerry, signer of the Declaration of Independence, the man for whom the gerrymander was named, and a two-term vice president of the United States. In the 19th century, poet and writer James Russell Lowell resided at "Elmwood." It currently serves as the official residence of the president of Harvard University.

These photographs from the 1894 report of the Joint Board for the Improvement of the Charles River provide dramatic evidence of the character of much of the tidal basin. The above view shows the marsh and bluffs near Watertown's Arsenal Street; the image below depicts the marsh in the vicinity of Watertown's Coolidge Street.

Two

Commercial Highway

Unsuited for residential development by virtue of its tidal character, the Charles River Basin assumed a decidedly commercial and industrial orientation in the 19th century.

Among the earliest manufactories to arise on its shores was the Watertown Arsenal, founded in 1816. Through a succession of wars, this important federal facility turned out guns, gun carriages, and ammunition for the American armed services.

In two major instances entrepreneurs projected ambitious industrial projects for the Charles River Basin that failed to materialize.

The founders of Cambridgeport visualized the creation of port facilities rivaling Boston's on the river's northern shoreline, in the vicinity of present-day Kendall Square. The Congress of the United States certified Cambridgeport as an official port of entry on January 11, 1805. While some progress was made in the first few years, including the construction of canals, wharves, and row houses near the northern end of the West Boston Bridge, Jefferson's trade embargo of 1807 killed the ambitious scheme.

Another failed industrial initiative was the Roxbury Mill Dam project. Its principal promoter, Uriah Cotting, believed that the Back Bay tides could be successfully harnessed to power as many as 81 mills. This grandiose scheme foresaw the establishment on the margin of a tidal pond of 6 gristmills, 6 sawmills, 16 cotton mills, 8 woolen mills, 12 rolling and slitting mills, as well as facilities for producing cannon, anchors, scythes, grindstones, paint, and other products.

The plan that was eventually carried into effect in 1821 involved the construction of a 50-foot-wide dam/toll road (present-day Beacon Street) between Charles Street and Sewall's Point in Brookline (Kenmore Square), with a cross dam running out to Gravelly Point in Roxbury along the line of present-day Massachusetts Avenue. However, the Charles River tides proved to be a much-less-efficient generator of energy than Cotting and his associates had envisioned, and little industrial development occurred in the Back Bay.

Greater success awaited the developers of the Lechmere section of East Cambridge. Preeminent among these developers was Andrew Craigie, former apothecary-general of the Continental Army, and the builder, in 1809, of Craigie's Bridge connecting Lechmere Point to Boston's West End. By the 1850s East Cambridge contained a heavy concentration of commercial and industrial establishments. Two canals, the Broad and the Lechmere, were built to facilitate water transport in this most heavily industrialized section of the basin.

The construction of railroads on both sides of the basin enhanced the area's commercial and industrial orientation. In 1835, the Boston & Worcester Railroad was built on the southern side of the river, passing across the Back Bay and then skirting the shoreline through Brighton and Newton. On the northern side, the Fitchburg Railroad was completed in 1841, and the connecting Grand Junction Freight Railroad in 1851.

While this engraving of the Charles River Basin bears the title *Charlestown from Brighton*, the Bunker Hill Monument at the center would not have been visible from Brighton. The engraving does, however, provide dramatic testimony regarding the degree to which the tidal Charles had by the middle of the 19th century become a commercial artery. The men in the forefront are gathering marsh grass, presumably for use as fodder.

This 1905 panoramic view of the Charles River Basin at the North Beacon Street Bridge crossing contains a number of notable details: the Watertown Arsenal (top left-hand corner), the Boston & Albany Railroad's Faneuil Depot (center), and the Faneuil Watch & Tool Company factory (right center). The latter two structures were both located in Brighton. (Courtesy of the Brighton-Allston Historical Society Archives.)

The Watertown Arsenal was established by the U.S. Army in 1816. The main buildings were the work of architect Alexander Parris, who also designed Boston's Quincy Market. This 1817 engraving shows the rectangular stone magazine at the arsenal, one of the original structures. (Courtesy of the Watertown Free Public Library.)

One of the federal government's concerns when it selected the Watertown site for the arsenal in 1816 was its suitability for schooner traffic. After sounding the depths of the Charles River, Captain George Talcott, the first commander, reported that the Watertown site was "well situated for supplying the forts in Boston Harbor and vicinity." Here we have an 1875 view of a schooner tied up at the arsenal dock, alongside its gas plant. (Courtesy of the Watertown Free Public Library.)

An extensive complex of buildings stood on the arsenal grounds by the time the Civil War broke out. Prior to the 1860s the facility had been used chiefly for storage and for the manufacture of cartridges and wooden gun mounts. During the Civil War a foundry and a laboratory were established for testing the strength of various materials, especially steel, which had come to replace wood and iron in the construction of gun carriages and other equipment. (Courtesy of the Watertown Free Public Library.)

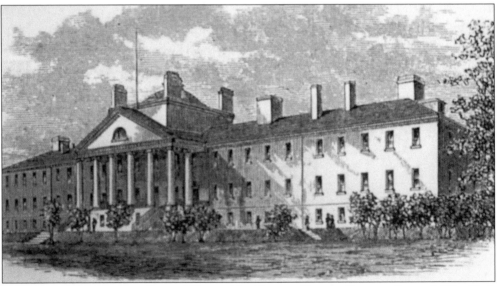

The original Massachusetts General Hospital building on Blossom Street in Boston's West End, designed by the renowned architect Charles Bulfinch, was constructed in 1818. The hospital complex, which stood quite near the tidal basin, had its own dock and lumberyard.

The Cambridge shore became a center of the publishing trade in the 19th century. A complex of buildings situated between Western Avenue and River Street housed the Riverside Press. Its history began in 1851 when Little & Brown bought the old Cambridge Almshouse, converting it into a book manufactory. The property was acquired by H.O. Houghton & Company in 1867 and expanded. The publishing complex was demolished in 1972.

Originally a hillock of upland on the river marsh called Captain's Island after an early owner, Captain Nathaniel Patrick, and later the site of a "public magazine of powder" (Cambridge's Magazine Street led to this stone structure), by the 1890s the site had become the most popular bathing beach on the Charles River Basin, the old magazine serving as its bath house. In this 1920s view we see the buildings and gas storage tanks of the Boston Consolidated Gas Company on the Allston shore adjacent to Cambridge Street.

The G. Fuller & Son Lumber Company and dock in North Brighton stood just east of the Arsenal Street Bridge (far right). A portion of the sprawling Brighton Abattoir complex is visible behind the bridge. Fuller Lumber was founded by master carpenter Granville Fuller in 1847 and survived into the 1950s. A highly respected local leader and businessman, Fuller served on the Brighton Board of Selectmen during the Civil War and in 1880—the same year in which the receipt appearing below was issued—became president of the National Market Bank of Brighton. (Courtesy of the Brighton-Allston Historical Society Archives.)

This long-distance view of the North Brighton shore, dating from December 1902, shows the river at low tide just east of the Arsenal Street Bridge. The Fuller Lumber Wharf (left center) and the main building of the Brighton Abattoir (right center) are visible in the distance.

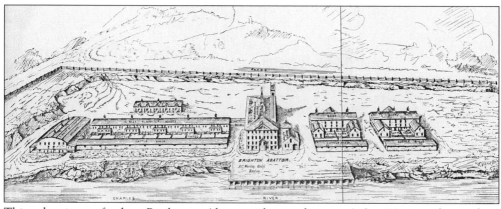

This drawing of the Brighton Abattoir by architect A.C. Martin shows how extensive the complex was even at its inception in 1872. The Brighton Abattoir was designed to accommodate all of the slaughtering activities within a 6-mile radius of Boston. As late as 1866, Brighton alone contained 41 slaughterhouses, which represented a major menace to public health.

The Brighton Abattoir stood on the river's edge between the Arsenal Street and North Beacon Street Bridges in North Brighton. The 60-acre complex had 1,000 feet of river frontage, allowing schooners and sloops to tie up at its wharves. Its buildings included a large rendering house and 14 slaughterhouses, 10 of which were arranged under one continuous roof. The abattoir closed in the late 1950s.

This photograph, dating from 1894, shows the indiscriminate mix of industrial and residential buildings to be found on the banks of the Charles in the 19th century. Here we have a view of the Cambridge shoreline west of the North Harvard Street Bridge.

The unimproved Charles River shoreline just above Western Avenue is shown as it appeared at low tide in 1903.

This view of the Charles River, taken from the Galen Street Bridge in the early 1900s, shows the Bachrach photographic laboratory (far right), situated in a building which had once been the factory of Stanley brothers, who in 1897 invented the Stanley Steamer. (Courtesy of the Watertown Free Public Library.)

While this 1908 view of Watertown Square post-dates the Charles River Improvement Project, it shows the industrial building (right) that housed Lewando's Cleaning and Dyeing business, one of the many factories that emptied waste into the badly polluted Charles River Basin. The Lewando's building still stands. (Courtesy of the Watertown Free Library.)

The tidal river's commercial character had been greatly reinforced by the construction in 1835 of the Boston & Worcester Railroad (called the Boston & Albany after 1867) along its southern shore. This view, dating from 1898, shows a B & A passenger train just west of Faneuil Station near the Brighton-Newton boundary. (Courtesy of the Brighton-Allston Historical Society Archives.)

The handsome Richardsonian Romanesque-style Faneuil Depot, built in the late 1880s, which stood on the Boston & Albany tracks in Brighton near the North Beacon Street Bridge, commanded an excellent view of the Charles River. (Courtesy of the Brighton-Allston Historical Society Archives.)

A Boston & Albany train is pulling away from the Faneuil Depot. The Watertown Arsenal is visible on the opposite shore in the upper left-hand corner of this photograph. (Courtesy of the Brighton-Allston Historical Society Archives.)

The most heavily industrialized section of the tidal basin was the Lechmere Point area in East Cambridge. Here a number of canals were built to facilitate the movement of goods. The 80-foot-wide Broad Canal was built in the 1806–1809 period by the Cambridgeport Proprietors as part of the ultimately unsuccessful effort to create in Cambridge a port of entry rivaling Boston. This canal was located just east of the Longfellow Bridge and was filled in 1966. The Lechmere Canal, situated northwest of the Museum of Science, which was excavated in the 1890s, was recently incorporated into the design of the new East Cambridge Embankment.

Three

River Crossings

The expanding and contracting tidal basin could be negotiated reliably only at fairly specific locations or river crossings. The earliest mode of public cross-river transport consisted of ferries. The first, dating from 1631, ran between the foot of Copp's Hill in Boston's North End and Charlestown. The second, established in 1633, ran between Gerry's Landing (the original site of Watertown) and a hillside in North Brighton known as "The Pines." The third, established in 1635, linked the village of Cambridge with the Roxbury Highway on the south side of the river, the main road to Boston. Ferrymen were typically local farmers licensed by their town government to transport passengers for a modest fee.

The volume of traffic on the Roxbury Highway had grown to such an extent by 1662 that a bridge was built to replace the ferry. Known as the Great Bridge, it was the largest public works project undertaken by the Massachusetts Bay Colony to that date and was paid for with public money. It was the only bridge on the Charles east of Watertown Square before 1786.

The transportation needs of Boston prompted the construction between 1786 and 1809 of three more bridges at the eastern end of the basin. All were built by private corporations and operated as toll bridges. The Charles River Bridge was built in 1786, replacing the Charlestown ferry. In 1793, the West Boston Bridge was built on the line of the present Longfellow Bridge, linking the West End with Cambridgeport. In 1809, Craigie's Bridge was constructed on the site of the present Museum of Science, linking the West End and East Cambridge.

As the road system west of Boston expanded, other toll bridges were added. The River Street Bridge, which linked Cambridge Street in Brighton with River Street in Cambridge, was constructed in 1810. With the extension of the Mill Dam Road into Brighton, the North Beacon Street Bridge was built in 1822. Highway construction in the northern part of Brighton led to the building of the Western Avenue and Arsenal Street Bridges in 1824. All of these structures were wooden toll bridges equipped with draws.

The building of the toll-free Warren Bridge in 1828 just west of the Charles River Bridge led to a fierce legal dispute that was settled by the landmark 1837 U.S. Supreme Court "Charles River Bridges" decision.

In 1850 the Cottage Farm Bridge, the last of the toll bridges, was built linking Brookline and Cambridge. Today the Boston University Bridge occupies the site.

The Harvard Bridge, the river's longest span, dates from 1891. It connected the Back Bay via Massachusetts Avenue with the Cambridge flats where the Massachusetts Institute of Technology would later be constructed.

Two additional spans were built in the twentieth century: the handsome Weeks Footbridge (1927), which links the Cambridge and Allston campuses of Harvard University, and the Eliot Memorial Bridge (1951) at Gerry's Landing, named for Charles Eliot, the great landscape architect who did so much to shape the character of the river frontage. In all, 15 bridges have been built across the Charles River Basin, of which 13 survive.

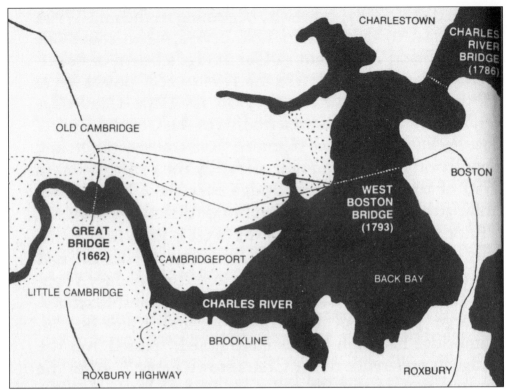

This map of the Charles River Basin in 1800 shows three of the four bridges that spanned it. The four bridges were the Galen Street Bridge at Watertown Square, dating from the 1640s (not shown); the Great Bridge at Harvard Square, dating from 1662; the Charles River Bridge (the most easterly of the spans), dating from 1786; and the West Boston Bridge, dating from 1793.

No authentic illustration of the original Great Bridge of 1662 is known to exist. Here we have a view of the wooden span (known as the North Harvard Street Bridge) as it appeared about 1905, with its draw partially raised (left center). Harvard Stadium in Allston is in the background.

This 1899 view of the North Harvard Street Bridge looking south into Allston contains a number of interesting details. Clearly a wider bridge was needed to the roadway on the Cambridge side (the present John F. Kennedy Boulevard). The picture shows the mixture of uses that then existed on the Allston shore. An industrial facility (the J.A. Heaton Coal Company) to the left and Harvard University's recently constructed Carey Cage athletic facility (dating from 1897) to the right are visible.

By 1913, the North Harvard Street Bridge had been replaced by a handsome new structure, the Anderson Bridge, designed by Wheelwright, Haven & Hoyt. Larz Anderson, U.S. ambassador to Belgium and an 1888 Harvard University graduate, donated the money for the construction of this edifice, which was named for his father, Nicholas Longworth Anderson of the Harvard Class of 1858.

The Galen Street Bridge at Watertown Square is shown looking west in 1906. (Courtesy of the Watertown Free Public Library.)

The present Galen Street Bridge is seen in a 1911 photograph. To the right one sees the opening of the Charles River Road, a mile-long and 26-foot-wide roadway extending along the northern margin of the Charles from Watertown Square to North Beacon Street opposite the Watertown Arsenal grounds.

The elegant 1,503-foot-long Charles River Bridge, the first to be built out of Boston, opened on June 17, 1786, on the 11th anniversary of the Battle of Bunker Hill. This wooden toll bridge connecting Boston with Charlestown featured 75 piers, a 30-foot-wide draw, 40 "elegant" lamps, and rose 46 feet above the bed of the river. It was also 42 feet wide and contained a 6-foot-wide railed pedestrian walkway.

By the turn of the century a steel bridge supported by massive granite piers stood in place of the old wooden Charles River Bridge. The new edifice, the Charlestown Bridge, also accommodated an elevated rapid transit line, installed in 1901.

The much longer West Boston Bridge, built in 1793 to connect Boston's developing West End to Cambridgeport, was a still more ambitious project. This 3,483-foot-long and 40-foot-wide wooden drawbridge cost a substantial $23,000. It was built by the Proprietors of the West Boston Bridge, a private corporation headed by former Congressman Francis Dana. In announcing its completion, the *Columbian Centinel* proclaimed, "The elegance of its workmanship and the magnitude of the undertaking are perhaps unequalled in the history of enterprises."

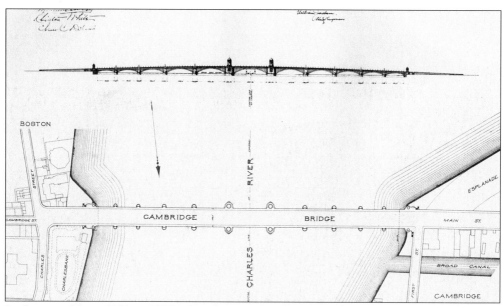

In the period from 1900 to 1906, a handsome 3,500-foot stone edifice was built slightly to the east of the old West Boston Bridge. Called at first the Cambridge Bridge, the span was renamed in 1927 in honor of the poet Henry Wadsworth Longfellow. The most elaborate and handsome of the river's 15 bridges, the Longfellow was designed by the renowned municipal architect Edmund March Wheelwright. Its four distinctive turrets were said to have been inspired by a bridge in Prague.

Here we see the Longfellow Bridge under construction in 1904. A cable railway carried concrete to the piers from a giant mixer. This photograph was taken from the top of the mixer looking south toward Boston. The cupolaed building to the left of the bridge is the Charles Street Jail. The octagonal building to the right was the headquarters of the Boston Gas Light Company. At the extreme right the old West Boston Bridge is visible. It was removed upon completion of the new bridge.

The completed Longfellow Bridge looking north toward Cambridge appears here about 1908. Notable details include the industrialized East Cambridge shoreline in the background. The gas tanks belonged to the Cambridge Gas Light Company. The Longfellow Bridge also carried streetcars across the Charles. Note the embankment on the right, built to accommodate the projected Boston-to-Cambridge subway line, which would be built in 1912.

This photograph of the Longfellow Bridge, with the Charlesbank in the foreground, was taken in 1909 from the Boston Eye and Ear Infirmary building on Charles Street.

Craigie's Bridge, also known as the Canal Bridge, which opened in 1809, ran between Cambridge's Lechmere Point and Boston's Leverett Street. Cambridge land speculator Andrew Craigie was its principal promoter. The 2,796-foot-long and 40-foot-wide wooden toll bridge cost Craigie and his associates $20,000 to build. Toll bridges were quite profitable. The total amount collected in tolls by the owners of the West Boston and Craigie's Bridges between 1793 and 1858 is said to have exceeded $2 million.

The North Beacon Street Bridge was built in 1822 to provide access to Watertown and points west for travelers on the Mill Dam Road Extension. The Watertown Arsenal appears in the background of this mid-19th-century engraving. (Courtesy of the Brighton-Allston Historical Society Archives.)

This *c.* 1909 photograph of the North Beacon Street Bridge looks toward Brighton's Bigelow Hill. A row of stone mansard-roofed double houses, dating from the early 1870s, lines Newton Street. The Boston & Albany Railroad's Faneuil Depot appears at the left rear, while a portion of the Watertown Arsenal's stone wharf is visible to the right.

An electric streetcar line ran along North Beacon Street and into Watertown Square. This c. 1909 view shows passengers on the old wooden bridge awaiting an approaching streetcar.

A new stone edifice is being built to replace the old wooden North Beacon Street Bridge in this c. 1910 photograph. The older wooden structure still stands to the rear of the new span. The photograph was taken from the Brighton side of the river looking northeast toward Watertown.

Here we have a contemporary view of the Galen Street Bridge looking west.

This *c.* 1910 photograph shows the old wooden Western Avenue Bridge linking Allston and Cambridge. The building at the center served as an office for the employee who raised the draw to accommodate the many masted vessels that were still plying the river in the years before the construction of the Charles River Dam.

This *c.* 1912 photograph shows the Arsenal Street Bridge at it appeared just before the construction of the present masonry edifice. At this point the stone piers and a part of the old wooden structure (right) were still standing. To the rear a part of the Brighton Abattoir complex is visible.

Here we have a view of the Cottage Farm Bridge connecting Boston and Cambridge about 1930. The original structure at this site, the Brookline Bridge, a wooden drawbridge, was built in 1851. Later the Grand Junction Railroad built a railroad bridge that crossed the Brookline Bridge diagonally. In 1906 the Brookline Bridge was rebuilt in stone at a higher elevation to eliminate the railroad grade and was renamed the Cottage Farm Bridge. Today the structure is known as the Boston University Bridge. The distinctive brick and terra-cotta building at the left center of the picture was built in 1913 as a factory and warehouse for the Ford Motor Company.

Harvard Bridge, looking toward Cambridge. Mass.

The Harvard Bridge, a 2,165-foot-long and 70-foot-wide span built in 1891, connected Boston's Back Bay via Massachusetts Avenue to the broad area of flats on the Cambridge side where, in the second decade of the 20th century, the Massachusetts Institute of Technology would relocate. This photograph looks north toward Cambridge. A portion of the Beacon Street Esplanade is visible in the foreground.

This view of the Harvard Bridge looks south toward Boston's Back Bay. Notice the streetcar crossing the bridge at the lower left.

From its inception the Harvard Bridge was a heavily traveled artery, as evidenced in this *c.* 1925 photograph. Here we see the Cambridge shore in the background, with the Riverbank Court apartments to the left and the main buildings of the Massachusetts Institute of Technology to the right.

Four

Filling the Back Bay

The most significant 19th-century alteration in the tidal basin was the filling of Boston's Back Bay in the 1857 to 1882 period. This massive project salvaged more than 600 acres for residential and institutional development. Upon these acres arose Boston's most prestigious Victorian neighborhood.

The Back Bay had been partially filled earlier in the century when the Mill Dam (now Beacon Street) was constructed; limited residential development occurred on the northern (water side) of the thoroughfare. The level of fill increased in the early 1830s when two causeways were constructed to carry the tracks of the Boston & Providence and Boston & Worcester Railroads .

In 1837, a Public Garden was created on the mudflats at the eastern end of the Back Bay. By the 1840s, however, the area west of the Public Garden had taken on the character of a public sewer. The building of the mill dam had obstructed the cleansing action of the tides; refuse was pouring into the Back Bay from the burgeoning city; and a public dump had been established on the land south of Beacon Street. Clearly public action was required.

In 1856, the Massachusetts State Legislature worked out an agreement among the City of Boston, the Commonwealth of Massachusetts, and Back Bay landowners that provided for the gradual filling of the bay and the laying out on the acreage thereby created of four east-west avenues to be intersected by cross streets at intervals of 548 to 600 feet. The central element in this grand design, conceived by architect Arthur Gilman, was to be Commonwealth Avenue, a 200-foot wide Parisian-style thoroughfare with a public park running between two roadways.

The gravel for the filling project was acquired in Needham, located some 9 miles west of Boston. A steam shovel (a newly invented device) was used to scoop the gravel into specially outfitted railroad tipcars for transport to the Back Bay mudflats. Each train contained 35 cars, with 25 trips being made in every 24-hour period.

The Back Bay's planners were especially eager to attract cultural and educational institutions to the developing neighborhood. In 1861, the Massachusetts State Legislature reserved an entire block for the Museum of Comparative Zoology (precursor to the Museum of Science) and the newly established Massachusetts Institute of Technology. Other major institutions locating in the Back Bay included the Museum of Fine Arts, the Boston Public Library, the Boston Symphony Orchestra, the Massachusetts Horticultural Society, and Boston University. A profusion of religious institutions also moved to the new neighborhood, including Boston's first, second, and third churches.

Because the Back Bay developed over a relatively short span of years, the area is characterized by a high degree of architectural unity. Most of its structures are Neo-classical in style. Within that general category, the buildings range widely from simple Greek Revival town houses at the eastern end of the district to large-scale French chateaux-like edifices at the more westerly end.

The Back Bay, with its handsome structures, rich intellectual and cultural resources, proximity to the city's business district, and socio-economic homogeneity, exerted a powerful attraction upon the city's elite.

This photograph of Boston's Back Bay was taken from the state house dome in 1858, before systematic filling began. The roadway to the right is the Mill Dam (Beacon Street). Notice the development that had already occurred along the northern side of the Mill Dam.

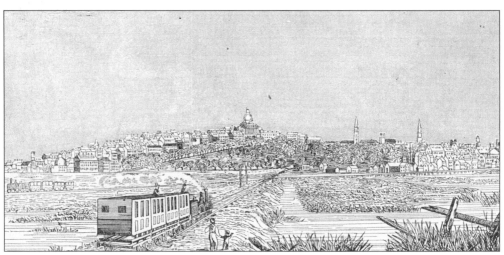

This 1840 view of Boston's Back Bay looking north toward Beacon Hill shows both Boston & Providence and Boston & Worcester trains crossing the marshes via causeways. The point of convergence of the two lines lay in the vicinity of the present Stanhope Street, just south of the old John Hancock Tower. The Providence Railroad Depot was situated in Park Square, while that of the Worcester Railroad stood near the present South Station.

This striking view of the still largely unfilled western end of the Back Bay was taken from the tower of Roxbury's Mission Church about 1878.

The land on which Boston's Park Square is now situated stood on the margin of the Back Bay. It was from this point that the British crossed the Charles on their way to Lexington and Concord on April 18, 1775. Here we have an 1895 view of Park Square looking west showing the massive Boston & Providence Railroad Station (right), dating from 1872, which stood until 1899. A copy of the Emancipation Group statue of Thomas Ball stands at the center of the square (bottom left). The Medieval-style First Cadet Corps Armory is visible in the distance (right center).

This engraving provides a southwesterly view of the Boston Public Garden as it looked in the late 1880s. The spired structure at the center is the Arlington Street Church, the first institutional building erected in the Back Bay. While the Public Garden dated from 1837, when a greenhouse and botanical garden were established there by Horace Gray, it did not take on its present shape until the early 1860s.

At the center of the Public Garden lies a 4-acre pond of irregular shape, now the site of the famous swan boats. This handsome stone and iron footbridge was built across the pond in 1867.

This 1858 *Ballou's Pictorial* engraving shows a steam shovel loading gravel onto specially fitted railroad cars in Needham, 9 miles west of Boston, to be used in the filling of the Back Bay.

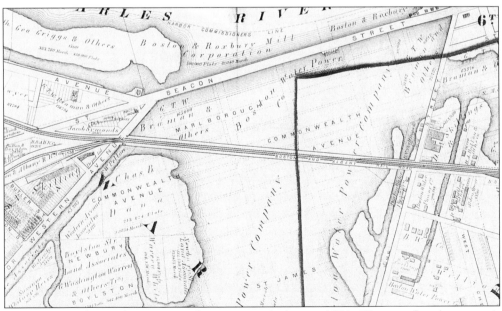

The filling of the Back Bay was a slow process. As late as 1874, 17 years after the project's inauguration, the western end of the Back Bay remained largely unfilled. Commonwealth Avenue between Hereford Street and Brookline Avenue in present-day Kenmore Square was then still subject to tidal flooding.

This engraving from the 1870s provides a view of Commonwealth Avenue looking west from the Public Garden.

Here we have a view of Commonwealth Avenue as it appeared about 1900 looking east toward the Public Garden from the vicinity of Fairfield Street.

Commonwealth Avenue is shown looking east about 1900. The cross street at the center is
Massachusetts Avenue, connecting to the Harvard Bridge and Cambridge.

The Arlington
Street Church,
dating from 1860
and designed by
Arthur Gilman,
was the first major
public building to
be constructed on
the filled acreage
of the Back Bay.

Boston's First Church, dating from 1630, moved from the downtown to this Gothic-style edifice at the corner of Berkeley and Marlboro Streets in 1868. Though ravaged by fire in 1968, the handsome bell tower and a portion of the cloistered facade were in 1972 incorporated into a modern structure designed by Paul Rudolph.

In 1867 the Central Congregational Church moved from congested Winter Street in the downtown to this building on the corner of Berkeley and Newbury Streets in the developing Back Bay. The magnificent Roxbury puddinstone edifice, designed by Richard M. Upjohn, is especially notable for its graceful spire.

New Old South Church, at the corner of Boylston and Dartmouth Streets in Copley Square, a flamboyant Northern Italian Gothic-style structure designed by Cummings & Sears, was completed in 1875. Its previous home, an 1816 stone edifice designed by Charles Bulfinch, had been destroyed in the Great Boston Fire of 1872. The original tower, pictured here, which was found to be leaning dangerously in the 1930s, has been replaced by a somewhat smaller tower of similar design.

Trinity Episcopal Church in Copley Square, designed by Henry Hobson Richardson in the Romanesque style, is the most celebrated of the Back Bay's grand ecclesiastical buildings. It was erected in the 1872–77 period during the rectorship of Philips Brooks as a replacement for Old Trinity Church, which was also destroyed in the Great Boston Fire of 1872.

Two additional institutional structures arose on a Back Bay lot bounded by Berkeley, Newbury, Clarendon, and Boylston Streets. In the foreground facing Clarendon Street stands the headquarters of the Museum of Comparative Zoology (precursor of the Museum of Science), founded in 1831. The building in the background facing Boylston Street, the Rogers Building, was the original home of the Massachusetts Institute of Technology, founded in 1867. William G. Preston designed both buildings.

The Boston Museum of Fine Arts, an institution founded in 1870 and situated originally on the top floor of the Boston Athenaeum on Beacon Street, came to the Back Bay (the site now occupied by the Copley Plaza Hotel) in 1876. This flamboyant Ruskinian Gothic building by Sturgis & Brigham housed the MFA until 1909, when it moved to its current quarters on the Fenway.

The Boston Public Library moved to a new home in Copley Square in 1895. This majestic Italian Renaissance-style palace, designed by Charles Follen McKim, provided a fitting home for the oldest major free public library in the nation. It was also the last major institutional structure built in Copley Square, thus delimiting the western boundary of the most attractive public square in the city.

Many elaborate and exclusive hotels were constructed in the Back Bay. One of the city's largest and most fashionable was the Somerset Hotel on Commonwealth Avenue adjacent to the Fens, built in 1897 according to the design of architect Arthur Bowditch.

Frederick Law Olmsted, the great landscape architect, oversaw the creation of a park plan for Boston—the so-called "Emerald Necklace" that extended all the way from the Boston Common to Franklin Park in Dorchester. Olmsted's master plan provided for the drainage and improvement of the Muddy River, which flowed into the Charles at the western end of the Back Bay. In this c. 1920 view we see the improved watercourse, rechristened "The Fens," at the point where it flows into the tidal basin. An overpass now covers the site.

Five

The River Transformed

By the late 19th century the tidal river had become a serious aesthetic and public health liability for neighboring cities and towns.

As early as the 1880s and 1890s, steps were taken to improve the appearance of the basin and to protect adjacent property from flooding, but no comprehensive improvement plan gained wide public support before 1903. Piecemeal improvement measures included the construction of seawalls on the Boston shore; the creation of an embankment on the Cambridge mudflats; the establishment, in 1889, of a 10-acre park on land adjacent to Boston's crowded West End; the establishment on the Allston-Brighton shore of the mile-long Charles River Speedway for sulky racing; and the building, in 1900, of Cambridge's Memorial Drive.

In 1894 the Joint Board on the Improvement of the Charles River recommended that the tides be permanently excluded by means of a dam just west of Craigie's Bridge. One controversial feature of this plan that delayed adoption was a proposal to allow new construction on the Boston shoreline, thus depriving owners of the existing buildings on the north side of Beacon Street of their riverfront views. There was fear also that the dam proposal might damage Boston Harbor and create public health problems.

The prime mover in the improvement initiative at this stage was the great landscape architect Charles Eliot (1859–1897), founder of the Trustees of the Reservations. Eliot was largely responsible for the establishment of the Metropolitan Park Commission in 1892. In 1919 the park commission united with other regional agencies to become the Metropolitan District Commission, with jurisdiction over all basin parkland.

The stalled dam proposal was revived in 1901 by two influential Boston businessmen, Henry Lee Higginson and James Jackson Storrow. The proposal for new construction in the Back Bay had been eliminated. The project won general acceptance with the appearance of the 1903 *Report on the Charles River Dam*, which answered most of the engineering and public health concerns. In the 1906 to 1910 period, a more northerly seawall was built along the Back Bay shoreline, thus creating a broad strip of new land (the Esplanade) extending from the Charlesbank to Charlesgate West, where Frederick Law Olmsted's Fenway (also then under construction) joined the Charles.

In 1908 a wooden dam was built across the mouth of the Charles, thus permanently excluding the tides, with the water level now held at a constant 7 feet above mean low tide. A permanent masonry dam replaced the wooden structure in 1910. The earthen dam east of this wall (now the site of the Museum of Science) became an attractive public park.

The Boston shore assumed its present shape gradually over the next 40 years. In the early 1930s the Esplanade was widened and lengthened by the addition of a lagoon, a sheltered landing for boats, and space for concerts. In the early 1950s, following the construction of Storrow Drive, the Esplanade was again widened and an enlarged system of lagoons, islands, and pedestrian bridges was installed.

One of the earliest measures taken for the improvement and development of the tidal shoreline was the creation of the Cambridge Embankment, a project begun in 1881. This 1902 photograph shows the embankment and flats from the West Boston Bridge at low tide. Note should be taken of the large number of people gathering shellfish.

Here we have a view of the Cambridge Embankment looking west in the direction of the West Boston Bridge, also taken in 1902.

This 1886 view shows the Boston shoreline east of the Charles Street Jail, a crowded, industrialized area that would be developed in the late 1880s and early 1890s into the Charlesbank, a 10-acre park designed by Frederick Law Olmsted and intended largely for the benefit of the poor residents of Boston's West End.

When completed in the early 1890s, the Charlesbank included a promenade (pictured here), two outdoor gymnasia—one for men and the other for women—and an intermediary wide lawn, intended chiefly for use by children. Unfortunately, this pioneer public park was eradicated in the 1930s when the Boston side of the basin was widened and redesigned.

Here we have an 1894 view of the Charlesbank at high tide, looking east from the West Boston Bridge.

This view of the sea wall to the rear of Brimmer Street at the foot of Beacon Hill was taken in 1903 when the river was still tidal.

This 1894 view of the rear of Beacon Street in the Back Bay was taken looking east from the recently constructed Harvard Bridge.

Soldiers Field and the Longfellow Marshes in Allston are seen before the construction of the Charles River Speedway in the late 1890s.

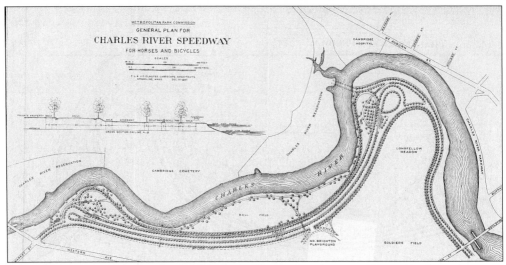

Major changes were made along the Charles River shoreline in Allston-Brighton between Market and North Harvard Streets in 1899. A mile-long raceway, the Charles River Speedway, opened here in 1899. This map of the contemplated speedway appeared in the 1898 annual report of the Metropolitan Park Commission.

Here we have a 1901 view of the Charles River Speedway, looking east toward Boston.

This 1902 photograph shows hundreds of sulkies gathered on the riverside course for the third annual "Speedway Parade."

In this c. 1900 photograph we see the unimproved Charles River shoreline a half-mile east of Watertown Square. Here at Lemon Brook opposite the Charlesbank Road, a major sewer overflow entered the river.

In this December 18, 1902 photograph of the river at low tide we see the Watertown shoreline to the left, including several wooden structures along Coolidge Street. Greenough Boulevard passes over the site today. Note the Mount Auburn Cemetery tower in the distance (center).

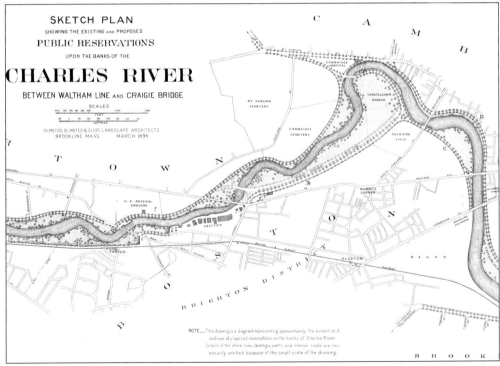

This detail from a 1903 map of the Charles River Basin by the firm of Olmsted, Olmsted & Eliot, landscape architects, shows the development plans for the area between the Watertown Arsenal and the Cottage Farm (now the Boston University) Bridge.

These two photographs, which appeared in the 1910 report of the Metropolitan Park
Commission, show the Charles River Embankment (or Esplanade) as it appeared shortly after
its completion. The top photograph looks west from the dam; the bottom image looks east from
the Harvard Bridge. While the lower end of the embankment was wide enough to
accommodate a street called Embankment Road, the upper portion, visible on the left-hand
side of the top view, being narrower, had only a service road for abutters called Back Street.

Here we see the sluices that provided access from Boston Harbor to the basin under construction in 1907.

This 1909 photograph shows the Charles River Dam nearing completion.

Metropolitan Police Boat House,
Charles River Basin and Bridge, Cambridge, Mass.

The Charles River Dam (on the site of the present Museum of Science) is shown here prior to its development as a park. On the left is the Metropolitan Police Boathouse. An arched viaduct, dating from 1909, carries streetcars from Boston to Cambridge.

This photograph shows the lower end of the completed Esplanade before the construction of Storrow Drive in the 1949 to 1951 period. The Hatch Shell, dating from 1939 and site of the Boston Pops outdoor concerts inaugurated by Arthur Fiedler in 1929, is visible in the distance.

Here we see the easterly portion of Nonantum Road under construction in Brighton about 1910 in the vicinity of the Brooks Street underpass. A train has just pulled up in front of the Faneuil Depot, a portion of which is visible to the right. The large industrial building left of the depot was the headquarters of the Rivett, Lathe & Grinder Company. The houses on the right lined Newton Street. The depot and several of the Newton Street houses were demolished when the Massachusetts Turnpike extension was put through in the early 1960s.

This 1922 view of the Charles River in Newton at the intersection of Nonantum Road and Charles Bank Road shows the newly constructed Perkins School for the Blind on the Watertown side of the river. (Courtesy of the Brighton-Allston Historical Society Archives.)

The Perkins school moved from its former home in South Boston to Watertown's 34-acre Stickney Estate in 1912. The tower of the Perkins school was furnished with a carillon whose bells could be heard miles away. (Courtesy of the Brighton-Allston Historical Society Archives.)

Here we see a 1910 view of the Charles River as dredged through Watertown just east of the Galen Street Bridge.

One of the most attractive and least traveled roadways on the margin of the river is Watertown's Charles River Road, pictured here in a 1903 photograph.

This 1930 view of the Charles River looking east from Watertown Square shows the recently completed Delta (1927), a handsome public square created by the razing of many industrial and commercial structures. The extent to which the southern side of the river in the vicinity of Watertown Square remained heavily industrial, contrasting sharply with the handsome Charles River Road on the northern bank, is clearly evident in this view. (Courtesy of the Watertown Free Public Library.)

Six

The Three Universities

Three major universities are located on the shores of the Charles River Basin: Harvard University, the Massachusetts Institute of Technology, and Boston University. While these schools came to their respective locations at widely different times—one in the 17th century, the others in the 20th century—all three had a major impact upon the appearance and character of the basin.

The oldest of the three is Harvard, founded in the 1636 to 1638 period in Cambridge. The first college to be established in the British colonies, Harvard was long the intellectual capital of New England. Not until the late 19th century, however, did it spread to the Charles River shore.

Harvard acquired two large parcels of land on the south side of the river in the late 19th century. One of these, the Brighton Meadows, was a gift of Henry Wadsworth Longfellow and several of his Cambridge neighbors, who bought the acreage in the early 1870s when they learned of plans to build a large slaughterhouse on the site, which would have spoiled their view of the southside meadows. The second of these gifts of land, Soldiers Field, was donated by banker-philanthropist Henry Lee Higginson in memory of six Harvard classmates killed in the Civil War.

Though mostly colonial in style, Harvard's buildings on the Charles are in fact less than a century old. Winthrop House and Kirkland House were built in 1913, while Dunster House and Eliot House date from 1929 and 1930 respectively. The Harvard Business School, on the Allston side of the river, was constructed in 1926.

The second of these riverine seats of learning, the Massachusetts Institute of Technology, moved from Boston's Copley Square to its new home in Cambridge in 1916. Its location on former mudflats presented formidable engineering difficulties for the builder, Stone & Webster, which was obliged to drive 22,000 piles to reach a firm bearing for the foundation of the structure. Designed by the distinguished architect W. Welles Bosworth, this massive Beaux Art-style edifice made of reinforced concrete faced with Indiana limestone is surmounted by a dome patterned after the Roman Pantheon.

The new MIT complex was dedicated in an elaborate ceremony that centered on the river. Assistant Secretary of the Navy Franklin D. Roosevelt headed the official reviewing group of vessels. MIT's seal and charter, as well as the officers of the university, were borne across the river in a Venetian-style barge, while thousands of spectators aboard boats, lining the shores, and on the Harvard Bridge cheered the procession onward.

Boston University, the last of the three schools to take up residence on the Charles, acquired its riverfront acreage in 1920, but the debt-ridden institution was unable to begin construction of its new campus until the 1940s. Further complicating its plans were public landtakings for the construction of Storrow Drive, which cut the school off from direct access to the river. Thus when the Neo-Gothic complex designed by Ferguson & Cram was finally built in the 1940s, it faced inward toward Commonwealth Avenue rather than outward toward the Charles River.

This engraving of Harvard College, which dates from 1726, shows the three structures in Harvard Yard that then made up the college: Harvard, Stoughton, and Massachusetts Halls. Of the three, only Massachusetts Hall (right) is still standing.

Here we have a view of Harvard College as it appeared more than a century later, in 1854.

The poet Henry Wadsworth Longfellow lived in this house at 105 Brattle Street from 1837 until his death in 1882. The Brattle Street mansion, dating from 1759, had served as the headquarters of General Washington during the Siege of Boston and later as the residence of Cambridge developer Andrew Craigie.

Here we have Longfellow in 1850 at age 43, seven years after moving into his Brattle Street mansion with its commanding view of the Charles River marshes. Longfellow wrote two poems celebrating the beauties of the so-called Brighton meadows.

When Longfellow and his neighbors learned in the early 1870s that a large slaughterhouse might be built on the Brighton shore, within sight and smell of Brattle Street, they quickly bought up the 70-acre parcel and donated it to Harvard College. It was on this land, known as the Longfellow Marshes, that the Metropolitan Park Commission later built the Charles River Speedway.

This 1907 panoramic view of the Harvard Stadium area contains many points of interest, including the old wooden North Harvard Street Bridge, the recently constructed Weld Boat House (bottom left), the 1900 Harvard or Newall Boat House (center right), and a cluster of residences that once stood on the site of the Harvard Business School, including the home and dock of farmer and wharfinger Emery Willard. Willard sold philanthropist Henry Lee Higginson the land that we now call Soldiers Field, which is the site of the Harvard Stadium. (Courtesy of the Baker Library, Graduate School of Business Administration, Harvard University.)

This 1912 view of the old wooden drawbridge at North Harvard Street is especially interesting in that it shows the draw partially raised. The bridge was taken down in 1913 to make way for the new Anderson Bridge.

The firm of Wheelwright, Haven & Hoyt prepared this architect's drawing for the Anderson Bridge in 1912.

This photograph of the Anderson Bridge was among the first taken of the handsome new Georgian Revival-style edifice, which was intended as a stylistic complement to Harvard's Kirkland House and Winthrop House, then also under construction on the Cambridge Shore.

The Newall Boat House, owned by the Harvard Athletic Association, was designed by Peabody & Stearns. This handsome structure, which dates from 1900, is notable for its unusual use of slate as a facade covering.

Here we have the main entrance of the Harvard athletic complex on North Harvard Street in Allston as it appeared in the mid-1920s. The 1897 Jacobean-style building in the foreground is Carey Cage, a gymnasium designed by two Harvard professors, Herbert Warren and Lewis Johnson, which was recently demolished to make way for new athletic facilities.

Harvard Stadium, dating from 1903, is pictured here. It was the world's first massive structure of reinforced concrete as well as the first large permanent arena for American college athletics. The stadium was designed by the distinguished architectural firm of McKim, Mead, & White.

Here we have an interior view of the Harvard Stadium, with its enormous 55,000-spectator seating capacity.

This c. 1930 view of the Charles River shore was taken from the Harvard Stadium. The completed Harvard Business School complex is visible to the right.

This panoramic c. 1955 view of the Charles River shore shows how industrialized North Allston was even at that late date. East of the handsome Harvard Business School Complex stretched hundreds of acres, formerly tidal mudflats, that were still being utilized industrially. The gas tanks (center) belonged to the Boston Consolidated Gas Company, while the two roundhouses to their right formed part of the sprawling Beacon Park Railroad Freight Yard. (Courtesy of the Baker Library, Graduate School of Business Administration, Harvard University.)

This westward view taken from about the same vantage point as the above photograph shows a shoreline devoid of industrial facilities, but conspicuously belted by Storrow Drive. (Courtesy of the Baker Library, Graduate School of Business Administration, Harvard University.)

This southern view from the Harvard Business School complex and Harvard Stadium, also dating from the 1950s, shows how close the North Allston residential neighborhood is to the university. One residential cluster, Barry's Corner, lying at the intersection of North Harvard Street and Western Avenue (top center), was taken down by the Boston Redevelopment Authority in the 1960s over strong neighborhood opposition to make way for a low-income housing complex. (Courtesy of the Baker Library, Graduate School of Business Administration, Harvard University.)

Harvard's Weld Boathouse, on the Cambridge shore just east of the Anderson Bridge, was built in 1907. It replaced a two-story wooden building built for the use of Harvard students who were not members of varsity crews in 1890 by George Walker Weld, who was a member of the Harvard Class of 1860. It was here in 1930 that the university's 300th-anniversary ceremonies concluded with a spectacular fireworks display.

This panoramic view of the Harvard University buildings on the Cambridge side of the Charles shows Winthrop House (left), the first Harvard building to open to the river, designed by Shepley, Rutan, & Coolidge and dating from 1913. Winthrop House's courtyard was inspired by England's Hampton Court Palace. To the right lies Dunster House. At the extreme left we see a portion of the Weeks Bridge, linking the Cambridge campus to the business school complex in Allston.

Here we see the southwest corner of Eliot House at the intersection of John F. Kennedy Street (formerly Boylston Street) and Memorial Drive on the Cambridge shore shortly after its construction in 1930. Eliot House was named for Charles W. Eliot, president of the university from 1869 to 1909 and father of the great landscape architect Charles Eliot. Eliot House was designed by the firm of Coolidge, Shepley, Bulfinch & Abbott.

Here we have a full view of Harvard's Dunster House, which dates from 1929 and was named for early Harvard President Henry Dunster. Dunster House, which lies east of Eliot House, was also designed by Coolidge, Shepley, Bulfinch & Abbott.

The Massachusetts Institute of Technology's Rogers Building, dating from 1863 and designed by William G. Preston, was one of the first institutional structures erected in the Back Bay.

Cambridge, Mass. The Riverbank Court from Harvard Bridge.

Riverbank Court, a Tudor-style luxury apartment building that lies at the corner of Memorial Drive and Massachusetts Avenue adjacent to MIT, dates from 1900. It recalls the period before MIT was built, when the area seemed destined to become a fashionable residential district. Now called Ashdown House, it serves as a residence hall for MIT graduate students.

MIT's Cambridge campus was built in the 1913 to 1916 period. This photograph shows the west wing under construction. Notice the Riverbank Court building to the rear at the far left of the photograph.

The Venetian-style barge *Bucentaur* transported the MIT Board of Trustees, seal, and charter across the Charles to the school's new headquarters in Cambridge in 1916.

As this 1928 view shows, the best vantage point for viewing MIT's impressive new home in Cambridge was Boston's Back Bay. The Harvard Bridge and Massachusetts Avenue connect the two neighborhoods. Riverbank Court stands to the left of the MIT complex.

This bird's-eye view shows the extent of MIT's giant Cambridge campus.

This 1930s view of Memorial Drive bears dramatic testimony to the area's transformation from an industrial zone of mudflats, shacks, and dirty wharves into a great scenic and recreational amenity.

As originally conceived, the new Boston University Charles River campus was to have included a massive administrative tower, named in honor of Alexander Graham Bell, the inventor of the telephone, who once taught at BU. Had it been built, the high-rise structure would have sat directly behind Marsh Chapel at the center of the campus and would have been one of the most distinctive landmarks on the Charles River Basin.

Here we have a view of Boston University's Charles River Campus as it appeared in the early 1960s, facing inward toward Commonwealth Avenue rather than outward toward the Charles River.

Seven

The People's River

The Charles River Basin afforded its neighbors many recreational opportunities even in the years prior to its damming—hunting, skating, fishing, swimming, and boating, among others. The earliest form of organized recreational activity on the basin was boating, as evidenced by the founding, in 1851, of Boston's Union Boat Club, the organization that built the handsome Swiss-style clubhouse that still stands on the Esplanade at the foot of Beacon Hill. Boating also took place at Harvard College. The great popularity of boating on the basin in the 19th century was evidenced also by the City of Boston's sponsorship as early as the 1870s of annual Fourth of July regattas.

With the building of the Charles River Dam in 1908 began a much more systematic effort to develop the river's recreational potential, as outlined in previous chapters. Until fairly recently, however, this potential was impeded by the huge quantity of pollutants that flowed into the basin from surrounding industrial and residential districts, especially during periods of heavy rainfall when the sewer system proved incapable of handling street runoff. Planning and investment in riverfront improvement failed to keep pace with the rapid development of these areas.

This lamentable situation began to change only in the 1970s following the congressional enactment of the landmark Clean Water Act, which furnished $200 billion for river and lake cleanup projects across the country. Meanwhile, the Charles River Watershed Association, founded in 1966, was promoting an increased awareness of the river's problems.

One of the biggest problems that confronted the basin's communities prior to the 1970s was the danger of flooding at times of heavy rainfall resulting from hurricanes and northeasters. This problem was solved in the 1974 to 1978 period by the construction of a new and larger dam a half-mile closer to the harbor by the Army Corps of Engineers at a cost of $48 million.

Today a cleaner Charles River Basin provides residents with a far wider range of recreational opportunities that includes walking, jogging, cycling, boating, sailing, rowing, picnicking, swimming, fishing, and even windsurfing. In addition, significant strides are being made toward the restoration of the river's wildlife. Now the basin's 18-mile track of riverside paths are in constant use in all seasons of the year. Outdoor concerts at the Hatch Shell draw huge crowds of music lovers to Boston's Esplanade. In October, the Head of the Charles Regatta attracts thousands of rowers and hundreds of thousands of eager spectators to the basin. In addition, a number of boat companies offer informative cruises of the tidal Charles. The modern basin is experiencing a veritable renaissance.

The future of the Charles River Basin as the city's single most valuable recreational resource now appears secure. The MDC is currently formulating plans to rehabilitate the parkland under its administration with a view toward increased public access and usage. Plans are also being formulated to integrate into the park system the so-called "forgotten half mile," the area between the old and new dams. Thus the future of the Charles River Basin looks very bright indeed.

The Union Boat Club was built to accommodate one of the earliest forms of organized recreational activity on the Charles River Basin. When founded in 1851 it was, with one possible exception, the first boating organization in the nation. In 1870 the club built the headquarters pictured here at the foot of Beacon Hill's Chestnut Street.

This *c.* 1900 view of children swimming on the shore of the polluted Charles River in Brighton, opposite the Perkins Institute for the Blind, underscores the desperate need for recreational facilities for working-class families that then existed in the basin area.

This 1911 view of the Esplanade's Boston Embankment in the vicinity of the Longfellow Bridge is notable for the attractive covered shelter in the foreground. The view also dates from the pre-Storrow Drive era when the Esplanade was more accessible to pedestrians. The octagonal building in the background was the headquarters of the Boston Gas Light Company.

The Metropolitan Park Commission, which had the responsibility for maintaining the Charles River Basin in the early years, provided a full range of facilities for the public's convenience, including this handsome refreshment shelter on the Boston Embankment.

This view and the next one of the Boston Regatta in 1912 and 1913 show huge crowds gathered on the embankment to observe the rowing competition. The building on the river's edge at the center of both photographs is the headquarters of the Union Boat Club on Embankment Road.

The Boston Embankment served as a popular promenade in all seasons of the year, as evidenced by this view on a December afternoon in 1911.

This bird's-eye view of the Esplanade and the newly constructed Storrow Drive, dating from about 1950, shows the Hatch Shell (extreme left), dating from 1939, which was built chiefly to accommodate performances of the Boston Pops Orchestra, conducted by Arthur Fiedler. The building on the river's edge at the center of the photograph is the Union Boat Club.

The 1959 Herter Center building that overlooks the Charles River on Soldier's Field Road in Brighton, formerly the home of the Institute of Contemporary Art, now houses the New England Sports Museum Library and Archival Center.

The popular outdoor Publick Theater stands adjacent to the Herter Center.

Here we have a contemporary view of the very popular Charles River Reservation, bordering Soldier's Field Road in Brighton near the Herter Center.

One result of a significantly cleaner Charles River is much greater fishing activity. Here an angler tries his luck in the mill pond behind the Herter Center.

This contemporary view of the old Charles River Dam sluiceway (now permanently open), which is adjacent to the Museum of Science, looks west toward the basin.

Here a cabin cruiser enters the basin from the old Charles River Dam sluiceway.

Cambridge's Magazine Street and Magazine Beach derive their names from this old powder magazine, which was later converted into a bathhouse for the use of Magazine Beach patrons.

Boating is a favorite activity on the Charles River and the basin is home to many boathouses. Pictured here is a yacht club on the Charles River Road in Watertown.

A recent addition to the many handsome boathouses that line the Charles is the Northeastern University Boathouse on Soldier's Field Road in Brighton, just west of the Herter Center, designed by noted architect Graham Gund.

Among the most interesting historical structures on the margin of the Charles River Basin is the Convers Francis House at the corner of the Charles River Road and North Beacon Street near Watertown Square, now the McDonald Funeral Home. Reverend Francis, a prominent Unitarian clergyman, presided over Watertown's first church for 23 years (1819–1842) before joining the faculty of the Harvard Divinity School. An even more famous occupant was Convers's sister, the noted author and abolitionist Lydia Maria Francis (Child), who lived here from 1822 to 1828.